TIME FOR KIDS READERS

we are NORTH CAROLINA

by Lisa Kline

Harcourt

Orlando   Austin   Chicago   New York   Toronto   London   San Diego

Visit *The Learning Site!*
www.harcourtschool.com

How many people live in North Carolina? Where do most of them live? How is the state changing? If you want to know about the people of North Carolina, the United States Census Bureau is a good place to start looking.

A census (SEN•suhs) is a count of all the people in a place. The United States census also describes the nation's people. It tells what races they are, how old they are, and where they live. If you look just at the data, or information, that was collected for North Carolina, you can discover some interesting facts about the people who live there.

The census tells us about people living in North Carolina, including those in Charlotte, its most populated city.

TFK 5

TOP FIVE NORTH CAROLINA CITIES WITH THE MOST PEOPLE

1. Charlotte
2. Raleigh
3. Greensboro
4. Durham
5. Winston-Salem

SOURCE: United States Census Bureau

More than 540,000 people live in Charlotte. Many of them own cars—and get stuck in traffic jams!

The U.S. Census Bureau conducts a census every 10 years. A census is held for two important reasons. First of all, the government needs to know where people live and who they are. This information helps the government provide services that people need. For example, suppose the census showed that a lot of babies were born in North Carolina during the past 10 years. That means the state would need more money for schools. What if the census showed that families in North Carolina own more cars? The government might need to set aside more money to build or fix roads. The state might also expect to have more air pollution from all those cars!

This is a census poster from 1937.

The census is also important because it determines how many representatives each state will have in the U.S. House of Representatives. Before 2000, North Carolina had 12 seats in the House of Representatives. However, the state's population has increased since 1990. So North Carolina gained one more seat in the House after the 2002 election. That is good news for North Carolina. It means that the state has one more vote on issues that concern it and the nation.

The U.S. government took its first census in 1790. Census takers rode on horseback to every home and farm. Today, the Census Bureau mails a census form to every home in the United States. One person in every household is supposed to fill out the form and mail it back. If the form isn't mailed back, the Census Bureau tries other ways to get the information. The bureau may send out workers to help people complete their forms.

It's important that the Census Bureau reach as many people as it can. This sometimes means going to great lengths. One North Carolina census taker interviewed a woman who lived in a cave. Another census worker tried several times to interview a man who would not talk to the worker. Finally, the worker baked the man some muffins. At last he changed his mind and agreed to be interviewed.

Once the information has been collected, computers sort it and do the math. Then anyone who is interested can look at the data. Businesses find some information helpful in planning for the future. Suppose the census shows that the state has many young people who might buy houses in the near future. That's good news for a company that builds houses. It might want to buy land to build them on.

What does the 2000 census tell us about North Carolina? It tells us that North Carolina has grown faster than much of the rest of the United States. It tells us that North Carolina is more diverse now than it was in 1990. That means the state has more people of different races and ethnic groups than it did in 1990. The 2000 census also tells us that many of the people of North Carolina have higher incomes now than they did in 1990.

In North Carolina, as in other states, more houses must be built to keep up with the growing population.

How many people live in North Carolina? The 2000 census says the state's population at that time was 8,049,313. (By the time you read this, the number may have gone up.) North Carolina ranks eleventh among the 50 states in population. Only 10 states have more people than North Carolina does.

Between 1990 and 2000, North Carolina was also one of the fastest-growing states. It had 6,628,637 people in 1990. The state gained about 1.4 million people in 10 years. That means North Carolina grew more than 21 percent. In comparison, the United States grew about 13 percent during those 10 years. So North Carolina grew much faster than the nation as a whole.

Will North Carolina continue its rate of growth? The answer will be in Census 2010.

TOP FIVE NORTH CAROLINA COUNTIES WITH THE MOST PEOPLE

1. Mecklenburg
2. Wake
3. Guilford
4. Forsyth
5. Cumberland

SOURCE: United States Census Bureau

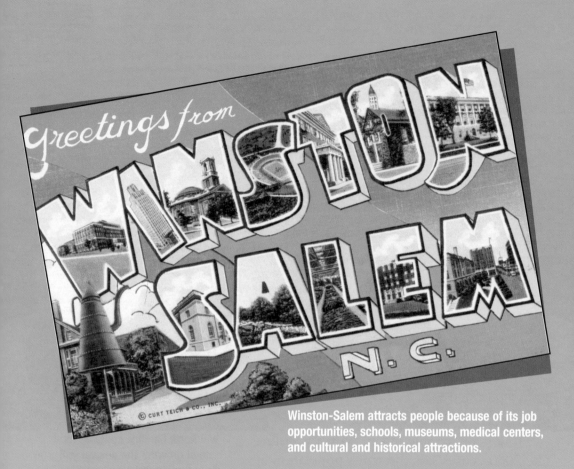

Winston-Salem attracts people because of its job opportunities, schools, museums, medical centers, and cultural and historical attractions.

The census doesn't tell why the state attracted so many newcomers. The attraction may have been jobs or schools or simply the beautiful scenery. North Carolina's fast growth means that the state will need help. It will need more roads, more houses, more hospitals, and more buses, for example. The U.S. government may give North Carolina more money to help pay for some of these things. Some will have to be paid for with money the state collects in taxes.

The census also shows that in 2000 North Carolina had 1,964,047 young people under the age of 20. That's about 355,917 more children than in 1990. So North Carolina will need more schools and teachers. More school breakfasts and lunches will be needed. More playgrounds and more child care centers will need to be built.

When the number of young people grows, North Carolina needs more schools, teachers, and equipment.

Hayley, 10, and her sister Cori, 8, moved to North Carolina from Delaware. "We moved because of our dad's job," says Hayley. Many kids have moved to North Carolina during the past decade because their parents found new jobs in the state.

One small town called Franklinville grew faster than almost any other town in the state. In 1990, Franklinville had 666 residents. By 2000, it had 1,258—almost double its 1990 population. That means Franklinville may get more government money to help with the services it must provide.

Washington

Oregon

Idaho

Montana

Nor
Dak●

So●
Dak●

Wyoming

Nevada

Utah

Colorado

Nebr

California

Arizona

New Mexico

Texa●

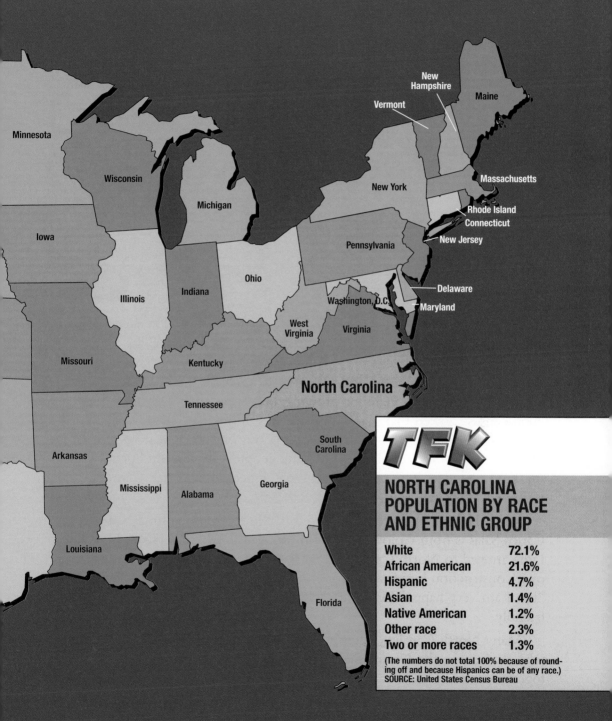

Minnesota

Wisconsin

Michigan

Iowa

Illinois

Indiana

Ohio

Missouri

Kentucky

Arkansas

Tennessee

North Carolina

Mississippi

Alabama

Georgia

South Carolina

Louisiana

Florida

West Virginia

Virginia

Washington, D.C.

Maryland

Delaware

Pennsylvania

New York

New Jersey

Connecticut

Rhode Island

Massachusetts

Vermont

New Hampshire

Maine

TFK

NORTH CAROLINA POPULATION BY RACE AND ETHNIC GROUP

White	72.1%
African American	21.6%
Hispanic	4.7%
Asian	1.4%
Native American	1.2%
Other race	2.3%
Two or more races	1.3%

(The numbers do not total 100% because of rounding off and because Hispanics can be of any race.)
SOURCE: United States Census Bureau

Hispanic people have their roots in Mexico, Central America, South America, and the islands of the Caribbean Sea.

Not only is North Carolina growing, but its population is changing. The 2000 census showed that many more people of different races live in North Carolina than did in 1990. North Carolina was one of eight states that had a huge increase in the number of Hispanic people—those from Spanish-speaking countries. The number of Hispanic people in North Carolina increased from 76,726 in 1990 to 378,963 in 2000.

Many Hispanic people have moved to North Carolina for a better life. Carlos Salas is from Colombia, a nation in South America. He and his wife, Ligia, moved to North Carolina to raise their family. Now they have their own construction business. "I work seven days a week," says Carlos Salas, "but I am very happy." Ligia Salas adds, "North Carolina is very family-friendly."

Many North Carolina schools have started special classes to help children who are new to the United States learn English. When they go to school together, children learn to understand and respect one another's cultural differences.

Although North Carolina has many more young people than it did in the past, there are more older people, too. In 2000, there were about one million people over the age of 65. People are retiring to North Carolina because of its mild climate, its mountains, and its beaches. Thanks to better health care, in 2000 the state had almost twice as many people over 85 as it did in 1990.

NORTH CAROLINA'S DIVERSITY

Race	1990	2000
White	5,008,491	5,804,656
African American	1,456,323	1,737,545
American Indian	80,155	99,551
Hispanic	76,726	378,963
Asian or Pacific Islander	52,166	117,672

SOURCE: United States Census Bureau. Not all races are listed here.

How have families in North Carolina changed since 1990? For one thing, families are slightly smaller than they were before. The average family in North Carolina has three people in it. Many families are headed by a single parent.

Families in North Carolina may be slightly smaller, but they make more money than they did in 1990. More people in North Carolina own their own homes than in 1990. The census also tells us that people in the state have gained in education. In 1990, seven out of 10 people in North Carolina had a high school diploma. In 2000, almost 8 out of 10 people were high-school graduates. The number of college graduates in North Carolina has also increased.

Some North Carolina people continue to work after the age of 65. This Cherokee woman makes and sells baskets.

In general, the people of North Carolina have been on the move for the past few decades—from farms and rural areas to cities. Census data tell us that most North Carolinians lived on farms and in rural areas 100 years ago. Just eight percent of the people in the state lived in cities at that time. Today, more than half of the people of North Carolina—more than 5 out of 10—live in cities. Fewer people now live on farms.

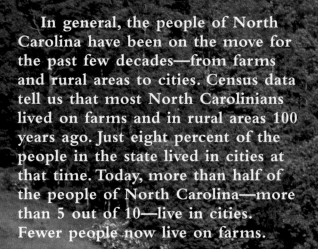

Farms in North Carolina produce tobacco, corn, cotton, and peanuts.

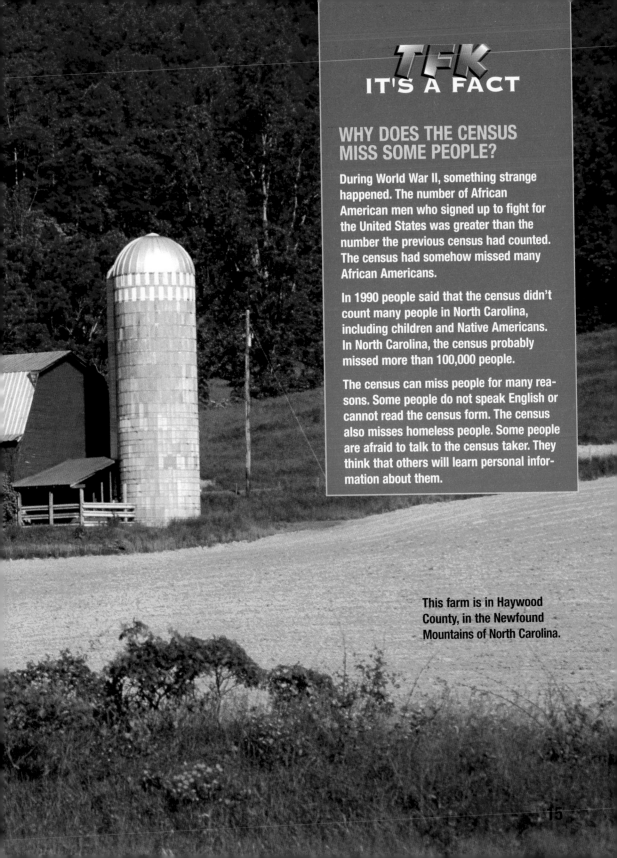

WHY DOES THE CENSUS MISS SOME PEOPLE?

During World War II, something strange happened. The number of African American men who signed up to fight for the United States was greater than the number the previous census had counted. The census had somehow missed many African Americans.

In 1990 people said that the census didn't count many people in North Carolina, including children and Native Americans. In North Carolina, the census probably missed more than 100,000 people.

The census can miss people for many reasons. Some people do not speak English or cannot read the census form. The census also misses homeless people. Some people are afraid to talk to the census taker. They think that others will learn personal information about them.

This farm is in Haywood County, in the Newfound Mountains of North Carolina.

It has taken thousands of people and billions of dollars to complete the 2000 census. Would you believe that the 2000 census is already out of date? Every day, new babies are born and more people move to the United States. One year after Census 2000, the Census Bureau estimated that there were already more than 3 million people in the United States. Every hour, the United States becomes home to 300 more people. More people means more changes for the United States—and for North Carolina.

Like the rest of North Carolina, the population of Charlotte keeps growing.